Copyright © 2018, Toronto
All rights reserved
ISBN 978-1-7750509-1-9

To Donna

CONTENTS

Semantics 9

Time and Sunlight 10

Time 11

Innovation 12

The Task 13

Expertise 14

Tomorrow 15

A Visit 15

Space-Time 16

Time-Shadowed 16

Desolation 17

Dawn 18

Renaissance 19

Enchantment 20

A Muse 21

A Cave 21

Psychologism 22

Aphrodite 23

Venus 24

August 17, 2014 25

Transported 26

Things You See   27
Conversation   28
Ma Ma's Pizza   29
A Night   30
Night Life   31
Sun And Phosphorous   32
A Peach Tree   33
Butterflies And Trains   33
A Park   34
The Mean   34
Once Upon A Time   35
Experience   36
Icarus/The Boy Who Fell Into The Sea   37
Constellations   37
One And Many   38
Fare Forward   38
Aphrodite   39
Donna   40
Analysis   41
I Remember   42
"The Other"   42
Hollyhock   43
A Pansy In May   43

A Bird   44
A Horse On Christmas Eve   44
Budgie Lost   45
Robins   45
Seasons   46
Solstice   46
February 13, 20 Below Celsius At Noon   47
Mid-Winter Apollo   48
Apollo   49
Young Man At Paper box   50
Tiny Man With The Big Voice   51
A Garden   52
The Runner   53
Street Player   54
Lady And Plumb   54
Talk   55
Laundry Man   55
Mother and Child   56
Sunday Afternoon   57
Alba   58
Julian   59
Travel   60
Roman Amber   61

Semiotics 62

Semiotics II 63

A New Year 63

Weather 64

Reasons & Causes 65

Compliments 66

A Moment 67

A Year 68

The Idealist 69

Sunlight in September 70

Dancer 70

Translations 71

Cavalcanti, Sonnet 29 72

Archilochus, 21 73

Catullus, 43, 51 74-75

Martial, Book one, 64 76

Book three, 4 77

Book five, 81 78

Book nine, 60 79

Book eleven, 57 80

Book twelve, 92 81

Baudelaire, Le Revenant 82

Wang Wei 83

SEMANTICS

Strong

Strange word

When relativity gets you.

The ant's strong

And fit.

How does fitness fare?

Well, strong's fit

And the fittest survives

Doesn't it?

And the poor;

They're strong too

Like the elephant.

Like the ant,

But are they fit

Without wealth?

TIME AND SUNLIGHT

From a-top the lake's old hill
The view to the sky
Appears
Blue draped
In the sunlight.

In the courtyard of Chinese tombs
An antique dial
Casts a shadow about 2;
And through its angular perfection
On stone
Time slips.

Beneath apple smells
Amidst conversation
Timed to a restless horse rhythm
And the longing to be home
One is consoled by the sun.

TIME

Looking for time,
We find him nowhere
Watching clocks, nor near the sun's way.
We subdivide his tickings
Till he's scarcely more than air:
He who gives dimension meaning
And counting to his tether
Makes infinity his contrary

INNOVATION

The fact's denied
The grand's demoted
And every embryo's
Reshaped
Coded
Structurally assimilated
To satisfy the economic motive.

THE TASK

Fearing what's obvious
We seek complexity
Avoiding directness
We circumlocute painlessly.

So more is forgotten
Little is learned
And the task grows more daunting.

EXPERTISE

I conduct no studies,
Sans science,
I state opinions breezily
Make pronouncements that never make sense
To the well informed.
I mumble old mythologies
Foolishly,
Taboos and wives tales
In several variations,
Seeming at times to be waking from a dream,
Shouting maxims
About affairs beyond my province
Concerning which
Only experts speak credibly.

TOMORROW

Phantom
Fly
Whatever you are
For you I run to the tip of a star.
Where I am and whence I've come I've devoured;
In my lust for a dream, a night-born apparition
I've lost the sun.

A VISIT

With her little rope
She jumps,
Disappointed to find
We've not stepped outside
To solicit
Her enchanting visit.

SPACE-TIME

Ahead the crowd steps to the sky;
Looking from side to side,
Future's to past as left's t' right.
Forward, times a line with past behind.
Where the toe tips back
Time forgets t' trace a now.
Like a diver gulping air
Perception wavers
Twixt what was an' what's t'be.

TIME-SHADOWED

The clock ticks,
The radio roars
And I like a counter moon
Reflect the times' momentary machinations.

DESOLATION

The air is wet-grey

And like it

I am free of colour

What distinguishes man from thing

In and out, down and up

Or you and me

Is one sea washed of relativity.

Time, space, place waver

As I flow through walls

Wet-souled

In this flux without fire,

Poured out

And resigned to this intermittent chill.

DAWN

Be not sad;

Sing not;

Shed tears when sun's brightest.

When winter

Smiles sunless,

Sadness

Begs quiet

To not say

What makes

Heart ache

Without end.

RENAISSANCE

Drifting to the path I plod so
ascetically:
Knarled leaves, brown on morning grass,
Cast me high from the inner flux.
Drinking deeply:
I behold the edge of things
And thank the gods.

II

After thirty-six hours of tension,
The light's been tuned to just the right angle,
Altering the scene as it glows through my
window.
I catch its swiftness
And like some ancient Olympian-
Exalted
I cast it far to the future.

III

Venus waking from seeds
Long cast from the father,
Sheds light, blossom-like,
Over city's winter grey.
Night past;
Soul loosed of coats,
Tight against self-cutting cold,
Flies to new air.

ENCHANTMENT

The spell that clears the mind
Draws the dreamer back
Earthward, sun-sprayed
Defined by brick and leaf
And the veil they make i'the sun
In the hush as grass waves;
And all that's disregarded returns
From under the shadow of forgetfulness.

A MUSE

This air
dry,
Burning and clear
Does not bite bone
But warms gently,
Skimming the skin
It touches the heart.

A CAVE

I came upon a cave,
An opening in a wall
And saw men seated watching
Shadows on a wall.
Shadows of varied shape
To a soft-sounding bell,
Flowed with a dark mysterious grace
Reflecting things eternal.

PSYCHOLOGISM

She insists her eyes
are irrefutable;
And I eager to comply
say I'm fooled.
Play oblivious to embarrassment
Don pointed cap and twinkle toes,
Assume a character void of schemes
Play whatever seems
against sense.

Physicians chortle diagnoses
Psychiatrists trace
My subterranean pedigree;
Say I'm mad
Solicit sympathies;
Still miss the intricacies
That complicate to free.

APHRODITE

Venus laughing sways summer branches;
Birds sing sweet-scented Cyprian air.
Lynx-eyed cat and fawning-grey wolf
Follow to Idaen pastures.

In Anchise's hut, Lady Love,
Lovely face turned shy in desire
Is stripped of bright garments and girdle
Shining jewellery of broaches and beads
And reclines on the backs of beasts
Her lover has torn from the forest.

In Rome's seething streets,
Cynthia tumbles her gown to the floor
From shoulders like marble
For her lover's eyes.

Above dust from his brother,
Paris plays with his lady;

And he knows she's so pretty
She must be Aphrodite
For Helen swears she's in Egypt.

Here in moonlight branches bristle;
Birds sing sweet-scented Cyprian air.
Lynx-eyed cat and fawning-grey wolf
Follow...

VENUS

Too queenly are they
Full of May
And guileless
I'd say
guiltless;
Wanting to orchestrate
All to their wishes
Rarely solicitous,
For their desires are all,
Others simply figures
In their blameless play.

AUGUST 17, 2014

They're nailing a roof on the house across the road
Near the tracks by the water's edge
Under wind-winding gulls
That climb at clouds just as playfully as comets
Off to the fathomless deep.

And on top of old St. Thomas church
Over there from Hart House
Miles west at the heart of the city
From that house that watches clouds, waves and wind-winding gulls
At the far east edge of the city.

TRANSPORTED

Sun Squinting across rooftops
Makes leaves silhouettes
On the dusky sky.
I take the rocket undertown
And fly through the night on a lightbeam
Till sun and sky set leaves a-dancing
In yellow-red
Wondrous godlight
Shining.

THINGS YOU SEE

By the tracks
Bouncing in the trees
A pillow like balloon in purple skin
Dances on the wind,
Set free to the south from the north some where
Straining on a string tethered to a tree
Near the train by the track.
Whence do ye come tiny cushion of air
Whose hands made thee fly through the sky
To be caught by a tree
By the train on the track heading east?

CONVERSATION

We talk till the weight of verbosity
Makes us stumble
Like enchanted gymnasts.
Worry in a chain of concerns preoccupies each
instant
Still, mundane matters
Nothing more-
And though the sameness
Of such situations
Masks reality,
Illusion, Time, Place,
Assumes the manner of a god.

"MAMA'S PIZZA"

I see a Mama's Pizza sign up ahead .
And I wonder who the real mama is
And what kinda pizza she'd make?
And there's a picture of mama
Right there up on the sign
Kinda 50's hair,
Sorta broad slightly smilin' face,
Class of Ernest Borgnine maybe.
But I can't stop thinkin'
What kinda pizza mama'd make
Would it be like the first pizza I ever ate
About an inch thick with just some tomato on top?
Does mama make that kinda pizza?
And if she does would they still be sellin' it in Mama's pizza store? (10.a.m. September 6, 2012)

A NIGHT

Sam talked to Joe
Cymbal hissed
And the drink man
Mopped the counter top.
Joe slumped toward Sam
The guy beside cried
And Sam saw none of it.
And I asked Bill if he didn't think knowing one thing for sure
Implied the certainty of knowing all of it.
And the horn man sailed a string of sounds over top
And the guy beside's eyes stared blank as stars.
And the night lady sashayed
onto an empty stool
Whose to know she's not just another lady?
So Joe told Sam to get her a beer.
And she laughed her thanks to Sam.
And the bass man traded 4's with the horn:
Tobacco smoke traded space with a gust of beer.

NIGHT LIFE

Here's no place for them wanting three
dimensional portraits.
Too much irregularity here
Weakness in disguise perhaps
but true
True as jagged glass -
Crash
cymbal shocks the moon blue
alcoholish mist
Anaesthetizing the humdrum
Like smoke cocooning
Steel mills
On a coal blue night.

SUN AND PHOSPHOROUS

Antique children of endless spring
Gaze blithely
Over timeless sands,
Mindless of their abandonment
To the fiery light,
Stilled before the flickering
Phosphorescent night:
Wizened visage
Powdered portraiture
Mildew blight.

A PEACH TREE

A stone I planted
Became a tree;
As if by magic
Or to defy inertia
or gravity
To fulfill its potentiality,
this essence
pushed up the earth
Bore fruit
And became a tree.

BUTTERFLIES AND TRAINS

An ancient tree hanging near earth
Expels a cloud of Monarch butterflies
Whenever a train shrieks by;
Then up like a mist, they blend again
With the leaves
As the train whispers into the western sky.

A PARK

At dusk scarcely audible, crickets twitter
invisibly.
At dawn above scattered wrappings, a squad of
Monarch Butterflies flutters menacingly.

THE MEAN

What one knows is what one thinks is so.
Only by deciphering principle amidst competing
egos
Can one hope to act ethically
Spotting the moral mark like the archer aiming at
the eye of the bull.
Only with eternal vigilance can one claim
adherence to reality
Lest agitated by desire
We say a cat's a lion,
A wolf's a hound.

ONCE UPON A TIME

A grove where a now forgotten
Deity was said to dwell
Maintains its fascination.
Mindless of anthropologists' explanations
Generations retrace the spot.
And in a moment sipping tea
Or through an early morning reverie
The sound of time and coffee
Graced by an unseen wisp of straying sun
Fashions spells in light-caverned leaves
Hallucinating Halcyon.
Youth's tasks, false starts
Lost in the years' spinning
Grow wild in their seasons
But through an Adonian ambulation
We return to replenish
High on a vague familiarity
A faint fragrance of ambrosia.

EXPERIENCE

Back in the good old days
Walkin'around
Takin' the stage
And poundin' the drum
From place to place
And gettin' to know
People all over town and
Way up north where it gets real cold like 40
below;
Down south to blue-white shores with
Beaches like snow
And cotton fields stretched to the blue;
Then up again
To the streets of old TO.

ICARUS/THE BOY WHO FELL INTO THE SEA

The Sky run turned dangerous
Because of the most unlikely surprises.
The horses charged ahead,
Propelled by an urge no amateur jockey could counter.
And the sun's well worn path
Seemed somehow obscured.

CONSTELLATIONS

They were made into stars
To compensate for their injuries
And to appease the consciences
Of their immortal tormentors.
Though we'll never know
If they're grateful to their benefactors
Making them eternally seem to guide humanity
in the guise of gods.

ONE AND MANY

The many made more imponderables
Than we could devise gods to apprehend.
Now that efficiency has quenched our naivety,
One remains where many reigned;
All but one has been explained
And he needs no questioning.

FARE FORWARD

Don't think that ease is man's natural state
Don't expect old joy as a prize that awaits.
He has no interest in what you say
When you curse his absence:
The moon follows the sun
Just to borrow his light
And never falls when there're clouds around
Nor should we
When what we're watching
Evades our design.

APHRODITE

Sky's so blue

Water and mind seem one

Love leaves garlands for the ground to wear,

Feet flying

None could deny deity,

And for him that would

There's no trusting

Just conniving and seeking his own,

No time to stand back

Mustachios twirling

Watching some sweet thing

Make the eyes of Venus shine.

DONNA

Your concern for age
and fear of lines,
Makes you rearrange your pretty face,
Draw curls -
Where shining hair quietly arrayed
Would gladden your noble visage -
Contrive new lines to some just dreamed image,
Though never finer than what you are.

ANALYSIS

It's clear

That where a smile appears there's pleasure .

When eyes a'mist with want

Contend with clouds

Sadness stares.

For surface says

Nothing less than what's seen;

Anticipating what's hidden

Gives meaning a merry chase.

And when with child-like innocence

One speaks one's soul,

What twisting of the heart says

What's said in full munificence

In truth conceals malevolence?

I REMEMBER

Two men with cankerous faces
And dressed in the same sad suits-
One assisting the other-
Blind leading blind through the door
Oblivious to, or sheltering each other
From the curious.

"THE OTHER"

Two factions
Both without privilege,
Without hope;
Without the means
To comprehend the
Calamity that engulfs them.
Each believes the other to be the blight that
consumes them,
The other that no mirror could conceive.

HOLLYHOCK

In my garden
As in the laneways I used to play,
A hollyhock nods against a fence
Patiently, without status or praise.

A PANSY IN MAY

The face, almost a circle
Of dappled tranquility
Making a place at its centre
Forever present
Even before snow withdraws into the mist
Waiting until it's acknowledged
In this tiny
Unassuming flower
So near to earth.

A BIRD

)w blankets the ground from corner to corner.
ranches spread black-grey shadows upon the
white.
Mirage-like amidst a tangle of dried vines
A charcoal-black bird pecks busily in the
branches.

A HORSE ON CHRISTMAS EVE

Guess who I saw today,
This icy eve of Christmas:
That lone brown horse who lives by the tracks
near Guildwood
Snow grazing
Happy to be free
Of the icy wetness that fell upon us yesterday
and held him hidden
And warm in his horse house.

BUDGIE LOST

"A blue budgie,
A friendly talker left his master
Who misses him very much"
So says the poster on the pole.

ROBINS

Spring's robins set free from melting snow
Fly from budding trees to the ground and back
Up into the windy sky.
But from summer's sun they seek the shade.
And hide when fall's first frost whispers
Fly – Fly –
Prepare for snow swirling through bony branches,
When no singing bird braves the brooding sky.

SEASONS

Summer lit trees
Fan dusty paths.
Winter bright waters glare
Off icy steps.

And those geese out there
That used to perambulate pompously in
Summer's fields and promontories
Now meet to bask upon the deep.

SOLSTICE

Winds rage round Rouge Hill Station.
Trees bend against the sky.
The ice-blue lake clings to the horizon like a giant tear
To see the sun begin his homeward ride.

FEBRUARY 13, 20 BELOW CELSIUS AT NOON

Nearly blinding
The star-white snow
Flashing back at the sun,
Almost warm
In the diamond bright's
Sub-zero stillness,
As Love fashions darts for spring.

MID-WINTER APOLLO

These days, January,
Make all light
Bright as a golden age,
Awaiting apprehension
In the chill of sub-zero wind
As earth passing the equinox
Approaches Helios from afar.
II
Mid-day smiles gold at the city's hub
And as air still with sunlight chills the breath,
Your heart flies round the universe
light years.
III
Janus, two-faced,
Snow-gold
Apollonian alloy:
Yellow-white
Taught as a bow
Strung on the horns of the moon.

APOLLO

Reeds wave and bend to the breeze.
The lake behind the trees
Rises blue to the sky.
Sun falls upon a dust-born path about an ancient tree
Whose writhing trunk and outstretched arms
dissolve into the dusty haze-
Waiting,
Watched by the waters,
Silence heard by the grasses;
Reeds whisper.
The enchanted air plays behind the phantasmagoria.

YOUNG MAN AT PAPER BOX, ADELAID & YONGE (9:20 am.)

Dear stranger:
Forgive my city
For locking its papers
And keeping your coin
Running you ragged without hospitality.
Still you're drunk
And you know it,
but as your friend said
It's the only way you can take people's bullshit.

TINY MAN WITH THE BIG VOICE at the Brown Derby

Short gentleman with the booming voice
You'd run up to the stage like a batter to the plate
Beaming as though the whole world loved you
Never complaining as they goosed you off the floor
When you hit the "Oklahoma" chorus.
I haven't seen you in ten or fifteen years.
You probably don't even recognize me.
And you, scarcely able to step six inches at a time
Even with canes,
Your poor long jaw almost too heavy for your tiny legs.
And your coat's hangin' on one button,
Half your flesh stopping the New Year air.

A GARDEN

Out there where squirrels
Spring birds and winter rabbits
Guard the grounds from human prey
All I've planted and laboured
To display, a patterned way;
They invade;
Sometimes to play
Among snowy conifers
And glistering rose leaves.
Always green my garden
Borrowed of wistful wishing, obscure imaginings
That fancy wants
The secret of;
Whence its coming
Whither its going
Why the prodding and the pruning that keeps it growing
From melting snows to drying leaves
from early spring to fall.
One morning still in winter's dreaming

Fantasy fashions a father's
longing made of spring-lit green, for
his little Tulia.

THE RUNNER

In the park
You'd run the winding paths
Kicking your heels,
And I'd laugh
Wondering what silly sprite possessed you:
Your face squeezed
Bright as an apple
Between stubby braids.
You'd laugh though offended;
And your eyes all aglitter with tears
Made me forget myself.

STREET PLAYER

Play your tune
plucked fine from fairy thread;
Let it thrumb to your dancing heart
Light with the brightness we've lost
Trudging ahead.
Play your sweet song
Play on lonely one
Play on.

LADY AND PLUMB

On the King car
A lady eats a plumb
Not too ripe,
Though plump as a peach
In her arch-backed hand.
Splashed in sun
She sparkles
In late afternoon conversation.

TALK

Let me speak

Not with a whisper

Snake-like, delicately hissing

But as a long loving roar

Like the sea

Rolling back to shore

As it washes the sky.

LAUNDRY MAN

Under a round-peak-cap

He wore the mask of a tragedian;

And when I mentioned my parents' trip to Italy

He spoke of the earthquake there that season,

Shot an imploring look at the sky,

Turned

And asked me why.

MOTHER AND CHILD

Tightly her hair adorns
Blue - grey eyes:
Sweetness warms them;
Care softens them.
She speaks, mindful of me
And the child she's left beyond the window
Lest its presence offend.
When my protests deny the need for such apologies
She beckons a tiny miss
Whispering baby things,
And holding something green.
Then sweetly this lady scolds her
For plucking a leaf.

SUNDAY AFTERNOON

Spreading shadow and light on surrounding walls
Sun sprays through the twisting curtains.
In the table you've just polished
The window glistens.

Foot in his mouth - dreaming
Sleepy cat curls in the corner
No sign he's aware that you've left.

Clock's pivoting pendulum clicks.
A sparrow chick chirps out a chorus;
And to travellers droning on high
March moans round the skylight in canon.

Through twisting curtains,
a branch tickles the light.

ALBA

Stay it's not the sun out there,
Just the moon
Glimmering 'gainst the lamp-lit street.
Let's just lie here.
Send the maids away
When Dawn's workmen
Cry through the early air
Wracking gears through hollow streets.

Dawn, be patient to-day;
Give fair Venus her way.
Fleeting as the firefly's span is she
And oh how rare art such scenery.

JULIAN

To Julian,
Apostate,
Philhellene,
The sun shone in threes,
And by its brightness
Returned Victory to Rome's senate.

Unmoved by the latest
Concerning the divine
He sought to reinstate the old gods:

A-bliss in a ritual dream: maids, men,
Beasts amidst incense,
He journeyed to Apollo's temple at Daphne,
And met only a priest
With a goose from home for the god.

TRAVEL

Beneath a cascade of sun

We clatter aimlessly

Through Milan

To the mountains,

The old earth

Scattered unrecognizably

Under oxide-orange tracks

And storage tanks surreally stained orange-purple:

Old gods out there

Shimmering through the miasma;

Soul alight twixt farewells and arrival

Still wondering where it's been.

ROMAN AMBER

In the amber afternoon
  she waits and watches
Acknowledging with cough and languid gaze,
  arrivals to the left,
Face in purple print,
  Alabaster
Gilded fast in roman amber.

SEMIOTICS

I know my manner

Of not denying my inclination

To behave like me

Moves you to conclude

I lack sympathy for your needs.

Despite my disapproval,

Presuming,

That under your auspices

My metamorphosis would set us free;

Don't take the rigour of my objections

For more

Than a sign of my determination

To resist whate'er might

Turn me against me.

SEMIOTICS II

I'm reluctant to tell you what I think
For what I think may tell you what I think of me;
So I say what comes to me
So that subjectivity
May not bind me to the mirror.

A NEW YEAR

Snows not quite melting:
Sky's blue;
Old buildings looked never so warm as now,
Blanketed like cosy old men watching Janus
conniving.
Tires hissing on sewer-steamed streets
Sound like their breath
As they sigh
With each puff of the pipe.

WEATHER

What do I hear in the wind,

a night cat's cry,

Branches banging black sky?

A storm,

a soul stirring,

A fiery whirl round planets raging for war?

Men mindless of planets and signs, in weather,

See simply wind, rain:

A natural disturbance.

Perceiving neither metaphor nor meaning:

The hand behind fortunes two faces -

They become like the wind;

Will - less and without wonder, they rage like the sea.

REASONS & CAUSES

Reasons are but patterns
Controlling our designs upon the world,
Names through which the will seeks visibility;
Lest in the darkness of its urge
Forgetfulness cloud the goal
For which activity began.

Hence reasons are like paths that intertwine
From then to now
But at any momentary place
Are limitless points in empty space
From which in reflection we may divine
In each intersection, a familiar pattern
of a recurring sign.

COMPLIMENTS

You say
My hair looks better grey
Tones down my swarthiness
You say
Making me appear less severe.

Oh
I suppose I should be pleased
with the compliment;
Still
I do wish I'd looked better
The other way,
So I'd not feel I should be pleased
With turning grey.

A MOMENT

Weaving a web of intricate design
Over air
A spider frames space;
Under shadows, a cat stalks his prey.

Watching the night
We wait Soon the sky will speak.

A cricket chirps and the silence sings;
Near the moon a moth flicks its wings
As gauze of Selena drifts over earth
Smiling Phoebus reclines on his well-wrought bed

Watching the night We wait Soon the sky will speak.

A YEAR

It was about this time last year
that you threaded the yellow-green banana peppers
and strung them across the wooden spice cabinet
over the old gas stove.

As the weather grew colder
we watched them wither
one by one,
turn orange-yellow
and finally a crisp Chinese red.

You picked the last two in January
When it seemed they might rot
had you left them hanging any longer.

To-day, as August runs its course
and that time returns through the first scent of fall,
the pepperless cabinet rekindles our year's
metamorphosis.

THE IDEALIST

My pockets jingle with change, silver dollars
And gold amulets.
My fingers glisten with diamonds
And delicious amethysts.
My home is a private store
For precious artefacts: paintings and more: -

In short, I possess all that's prized
For its potential invisibility:
Its infinite perfectibility
As currency.

SUNLIGHT IN SEPTEMBER

The rain's stopped,

And the cooling air

In a rush against yellowing leaves

Sends the setting sun

Shimmering and blinking through the curtains.

DANCER

Little lady

Like the moon and changing

Round and dancing

As the seasons

Full of light and dark

And laughing at the sun.

TRANSLATIONS

CAVALCANTI

SONNET 29

Dante heart's messenger, a sigh,
Assailed me suddenly as I lay sleeping.
Trembling I awoke in a mote companion to Love.
Turning I saw the maid of Mona Lagia come crying
" Pity help if you can",
I forced such courage of Pity
That I dared face Love sharpening his darts
And demanded he explain his hurts
And like this he replied:
Tell the maid the lady awaits his pleasure
And if he'd not believe it, let him watch her eyes.

ARCHILOCUS,
Greek Elegy and Iambus II :

21

With my spear I knead my bread.
My Ismaric wine I drink,
Reclining with my spear.

CATULLUS

43

Hello girl with the not too little nose
Nor pretty feet, nor black eyes
Nor slender fingers or caressable ears
And not too elegant diction,
Friend of Formian deadbeats.
Don't our provincials fable your beauty?
Don't they compare you to my Lesbia?
Bah! tasteless and ignorant age!

51

That man seems a god
Greater than the gods, dare I say,
Who sits opposite you endlessly gazing at you and
Listening to your sweet laughter.
Oh! such misery assails my senses
At just the sight of you.
Nothing is more wonderful to me than the sound of your voice.
My tongue's in a torpor stilled by a raging passion,
And I hear only the tingling of mine own ears;
The light of my eyes is enshrouded in a dark night.
The pleasures of inaction Catullus, have ensnared you;
You revel in it; show it in your every move -
Inaction Catullus, the destroyer of kings and magnificent cities!

MARTIAL

BOOK ONE, 64

Everyone knows Fabula
That you are a rich beautiful young lady
It's true!
Who could deny it?
But when you praise yourself too much
You are neither rich, nor beautiful
Nor a lady.

BOOK THREE, 4

Go to Rome book: if asked where you're from
Say somewhere near the Aemilian Way
If questioned about the country or the city where
I stay
Say that I have permission to live in Foro Corneli
If anyone asks why I left Rome
Admit everything: tell them "He's unable to
endure the shallowness of the toga ed crowd."
If someone demands to know when I'll return
Say "He left a poet, but will return when he can
play the lyre.

"GOD BLESS THE CHILD"

written in 20th century America by Billie Holiday and Arthur Herzog junior echoes sentiments of a couplet written in Latin by Martial in first century Rome.

"Them that's got shall get
Them that's not shall lose"(Holiday&Herzog)

BOOK FIVE, 81

"If you are a pauper now Aemellius, you will always be a pauper.
For nowadays no one gets anything unless they're rich." (Martial)

BOOK NINE, 60

Whether you blossomed in the fields about Paestum or Tiber,
Or your blooms be-decked the plains of Tusculum;
Whether a farmer's wife snipped you from a Praenestine garden where you were the glory of the Campanian countryside:
That this chaplet may seem more beauteous to our Sabino,
Let him think you 're from my place at Nomentano.

BOOK ELEVEN, 57

Do you wonder, learned Severus, why I send you
verses when I invite you to dine?
Jupiter lives luxuriously on ambrosia and nectar;
and yet we propitiate him with raw entrails and
plain wine.
And Seeing that by the favour of heaven every
blessing is yours,
Why would you want what you already have?

BOOK TWELVE, 92

You often ask me, Priscus, what sort of person
I'd be, if I were suddenly rich and powerful.
Who can say what his future conduct would be?
Tell me Pricus, if you were suddenly a lion,
What sort of beast would you be?

CHARLES BAUDELAIRE

LE REVENANT

Looking like an angel to the wild eyed
I will enter your lair,
Gliding about you silently
With other shadows of the night.

To you my dark one
I'll give kisses cold as the moon
And caresses of serpents
Slithering about a ditch.

And as morning's greyish haze arrives
In the place where I did lie
That iron cold night,
You'll find an empty space.

For as others may out of tenderness
Your vitality and your youth revere ,
I would rule by fear.

WANG WEI (Early Tang Dynasty 699-759)

PARTING

Farewells amidst mountains end;
Day fall shuts my brushwood door.

Grass greens again in spring:

My grandson may return.

MEMORIES

This man's from my old home town
Must know something about how things are back there.
When the sun shines up through my window curtains,
Can you see the winter plum tree flowering yet?

Manufactured by Amazon.ca
Bolton, ON